BEHIND THE SCENES
AIRPORTS

BEHIND THE SCENES
AIRPORTS

CONSULTANT LAURENCE HARDISTY

ILLUSTRATED BY MAXIM USIK

CONTENTS

WELCOME TO THE AIRPORT
P. 6 - WHAT'S BEHIND THE SCENES?

DEPARTURES
P. 8 - WHERE'S EVERYBODY GOING?

LUGGAGE & CARGO
P. 12 - DO SUITCASES GET MIXED UP?

SECURITY & PASSPORTS
P. 18 - CAN A BODY SCANNER SEE ME NAKED?

ON THE RAMP
P. 22 - IS THE RAMP ACTUALLY A RAMP?

IN THE COCKPIT
P. 28 – WHAT DOES THIS SWITCH DO?

THE CONTROL TOWER
P. 32 – WHAT DO AIR TRAFFIC CONTROLLERS DO?

ON THE RUNWAY
P. 36 – WHAT SIDE OF THE ROAD DO PLANES DRIVE ON?

ON BOARD THE PLANE
P. 42 – WHY CAN'T WE FLY WITH THE WINDOWS OPEN?

P. 46 – GLOSSARY
P. 47 – INDEX

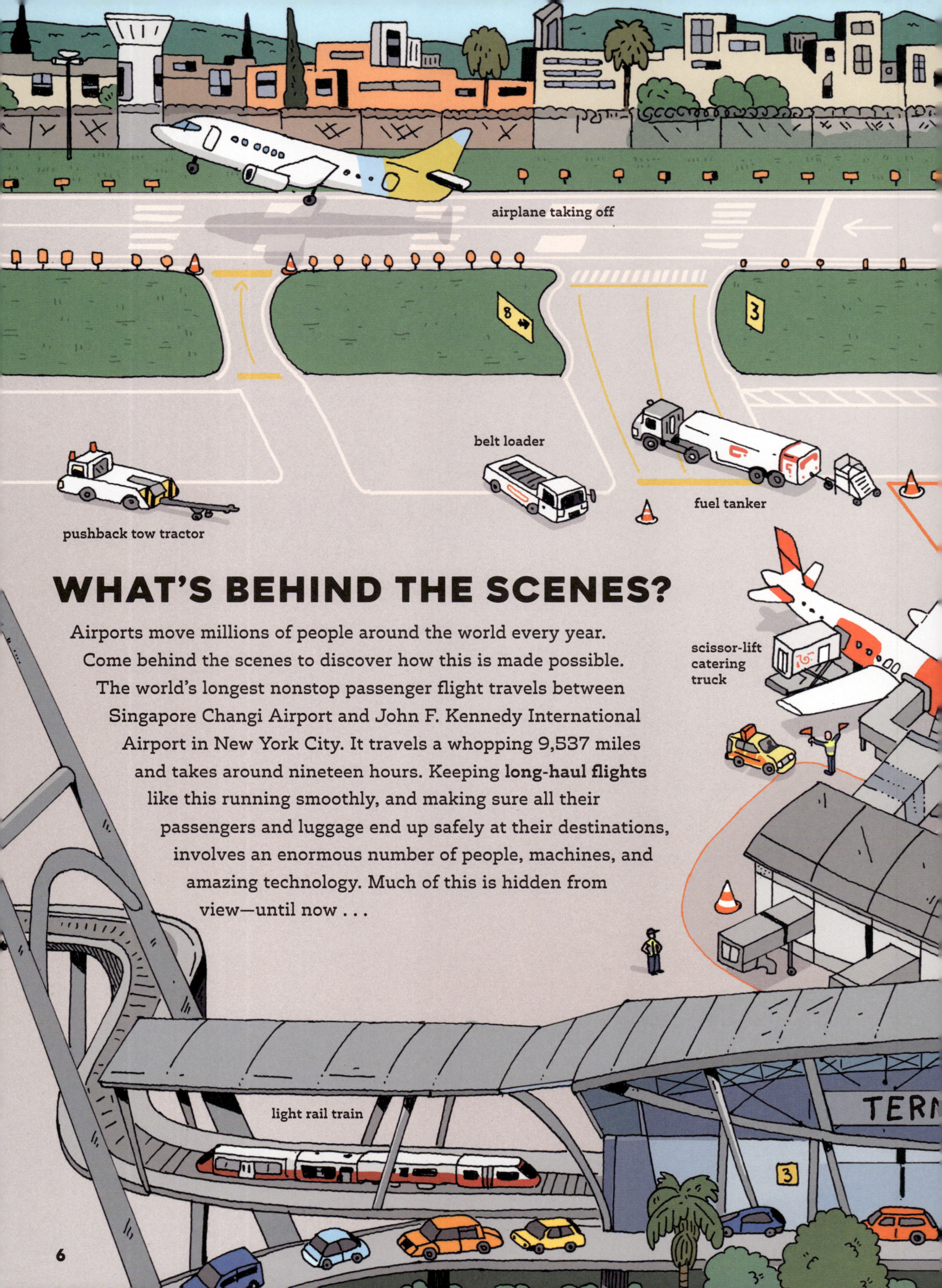

airplane taking off

pushback tow tractor

belt loader

fuel tanker

scissor-lift catering truck

WHAT'S BEHIND THE SCENES?

Airports move millions of people around the world every year. Come behind the scenes to discover how this is made possible. The world's longest nonstop passenger flight travels between Singapore Changi Airport and John F. Kennedy International Airport in New York City. It travels a whopping 9,537 miles and takes around nineteen hours. Keeping **long-haul flights** like this running smoothly, and making sure all their passengers and luggage end up safely at their destinations, involves an enormous number of people, machines, and amazing technology. Much of this is hidden from view—until now . . .

light rail train

DEPARTURE TERMINAL

WHERE'S EVERYBODY GOING?

On average there are 9,728 airplanes in the sky at any given time. Planes are crisscrossing the world constantly. The question is— where's everybody going? People travel for all kinds of reasons— work trips, vacations, to visit family abroad, or to discover somewhere new. The departure **terminal** is where everyone starts their journey. The departures information board lists the times and destinations that each flight departs throughout the day, and is updated every sixty seconds using flight data that is collected by the airport's information **database servers**.

WHY DO I HAVE TO ARRIVE SO EARLY?

Some airports have as many as 275,000 people passing through them every day. That's the population of an entire city! The way airports deal with this much human traffic is to create a lot of space for lines and to ask passengers to arrive early. Although three hours sounds like a long time to get from the **check-in** desk to your plane, you might be surprised by how little time you have to spare . . .

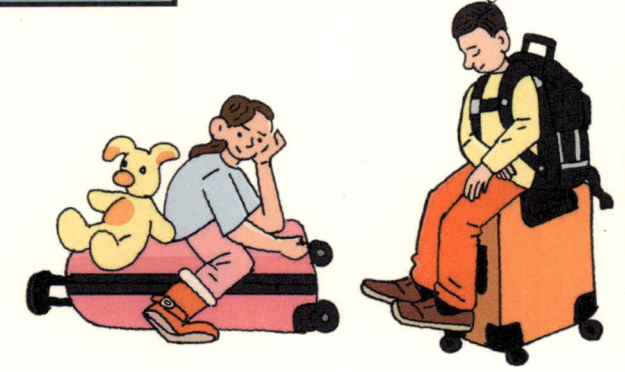

START HERE

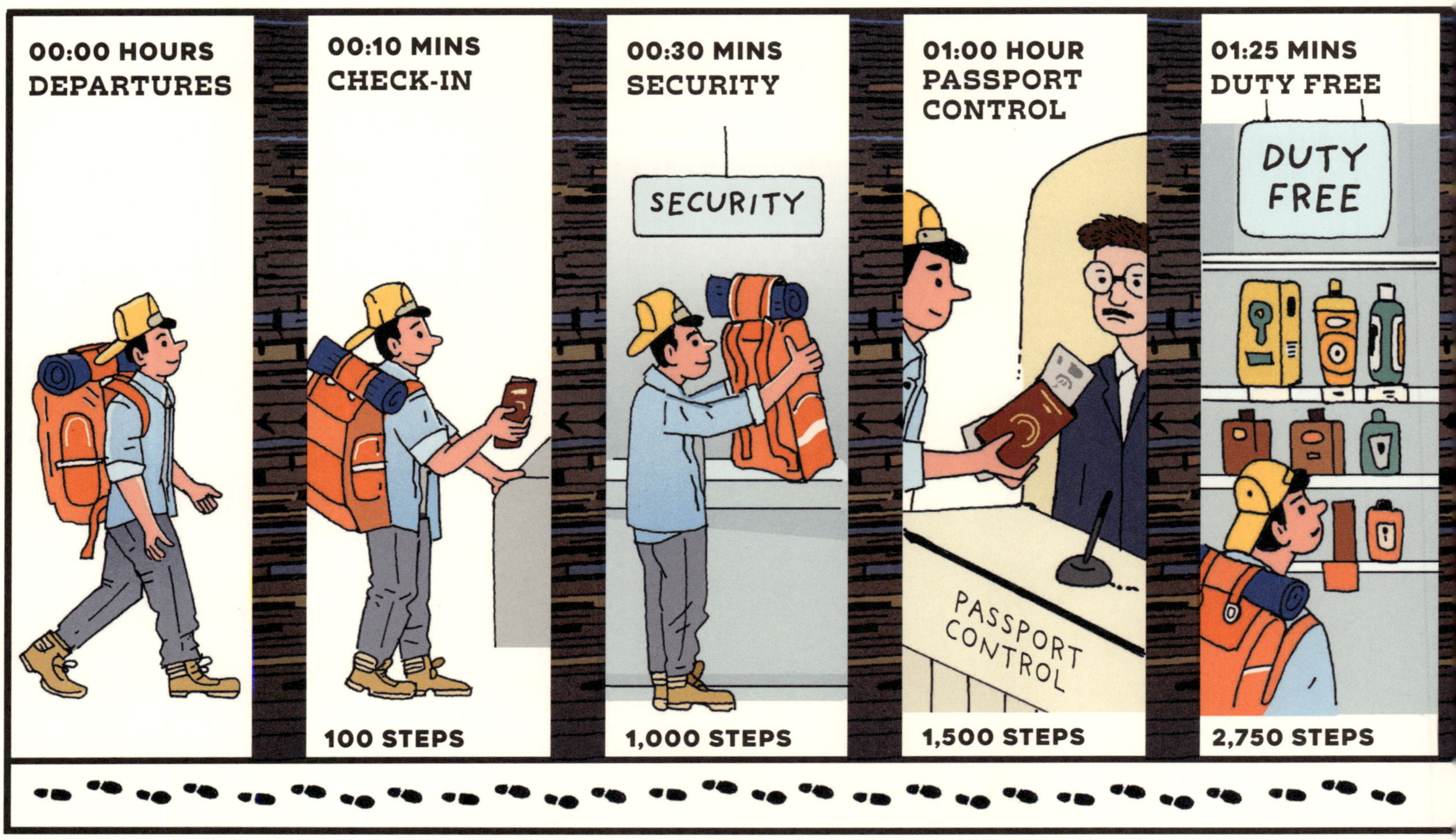
00:00 HOURS DEPARTURES
00:10 MINS CHECK-IN
100 STEPS
00:30 MINS SECURITY
SECURITY
1,000 STEPS
01:00 HOUR PASSPORT CONTROL
PASSPORT CONTROL
1,500 STEPS
01:25 MINS DUTY FREE
DUTY FREE
2,750 STEPS

CAN I FLY BACK IN TIME?

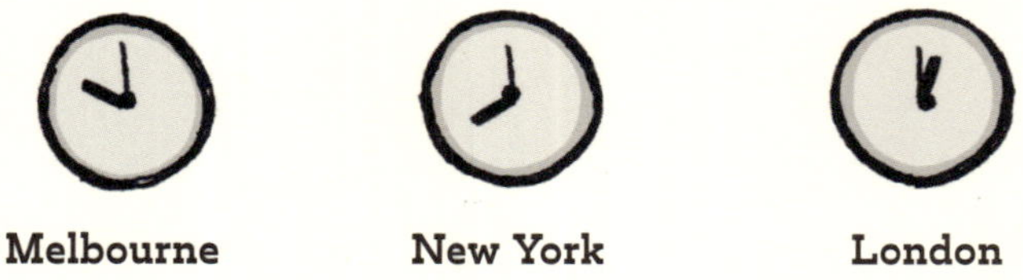
Melbourne
New York
London

Airports have international clocks on the wall to show what time it is in different cities around the world. These are called "time zones." For example, if you're reading this book at bedtime in Melbourne, Australia, it will be lunchtime in London, UK and breakfast time in New York, US on the same day. So what happens when you fly from one time zone to another? You time travel!

ARRIVE
Los Angeles
Friday
3pm
LA
LOS ANGELES

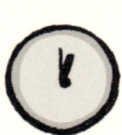

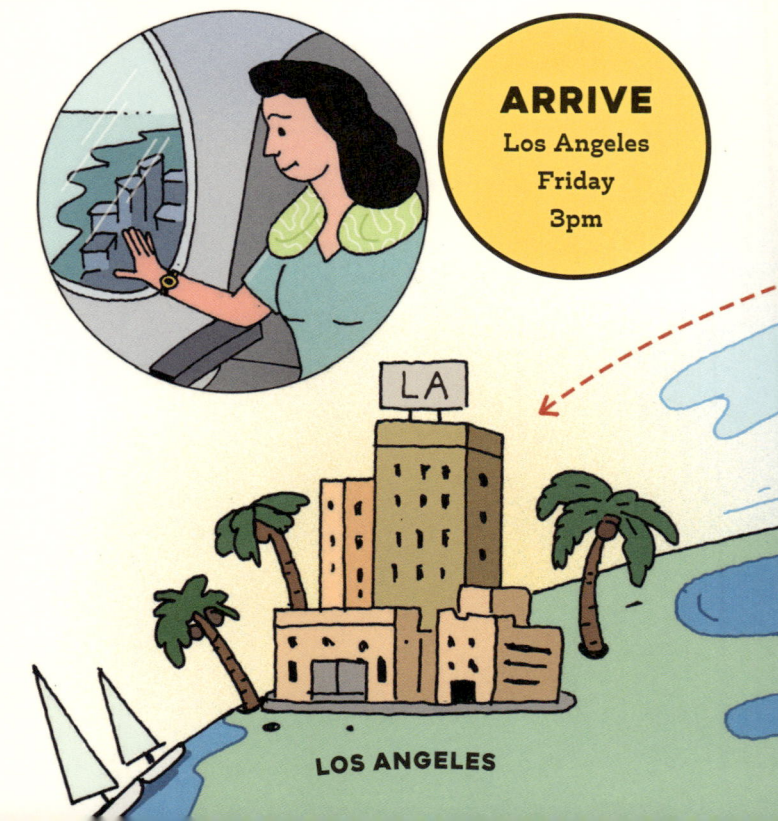

WHO GETS TO RIDE IN THE GOLF CARTS?

Because international airports are so large, you might need to walk as many as 4,000 steps between arriving at the airport and **boarding** the plane. That's 2 miles in total! If you have limited mobility or are unable to walk that far in one go, let your airline know. They will arrange to pick you up in a shuttle cart and fast-track your journey.

DEPARTURES

01:40 MINS DEPARTURE LOUNGE	02:00 HOURS DEPARTURE GATE	02:20 MINS RAMP	02:40 MINS AIRPLANE	03:00 HOURS TAKEOFF
3,000 STEPS	3,500 STEPS	3,750 STEPS	4,000 STEPS	YOU'VE WALKED 2 MILES IN TOTAL

FLIGHT TAKES 10 HOURS

DEPART Tokyo Friday 9pm

TOKYO

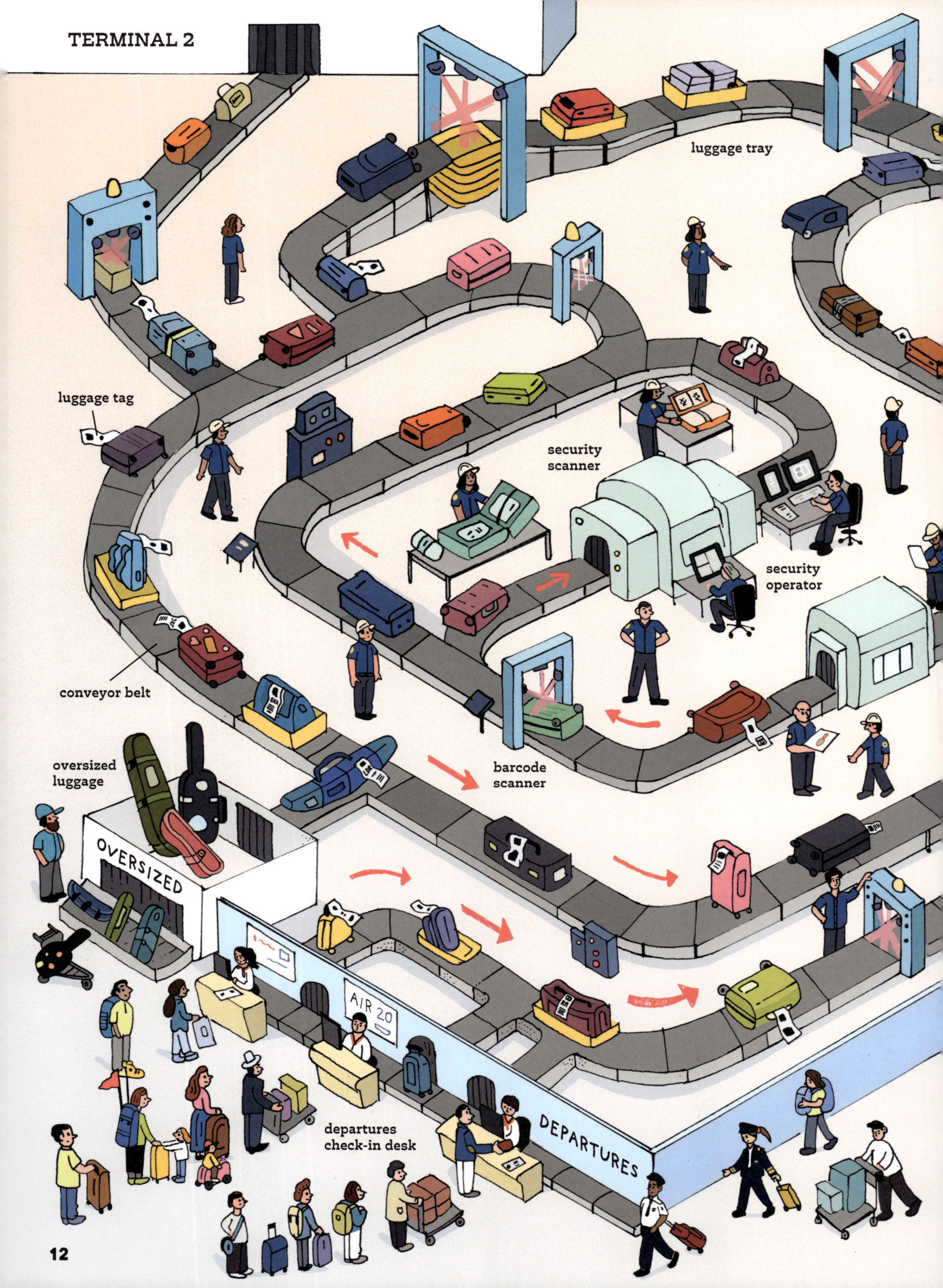

DO SUITCASES GET MIXED UP?

Airports use automatic systems to move and locate luggage around an airport. At check-in, every piece of luggage is given a tag printed with a barcode. The barcode indicates what flight a bag is bound for and its destination. The bag is placed on a **conveyor belt** and enters a large network of tracks, sensors, and sorters underneath the airport building. When there are a lot of bags passing through the system it is possible for barcodes to be misread. When this happens, staff sort the bags manually.

WHAT CAN A SECURITY SCANNER DETECT?

Every bag passes through a security scanner called an explosive detection system machine, or EDS. The scanner uses different types of X-rays to identify materials that could easily ignite or explode. This includes lithium batteries, flammable liquids and solids, and compressed and liquefied gases. Bags that contain dangerous items trigger an alert and are led onto a different track to be analyzed in more detail by a security operator.

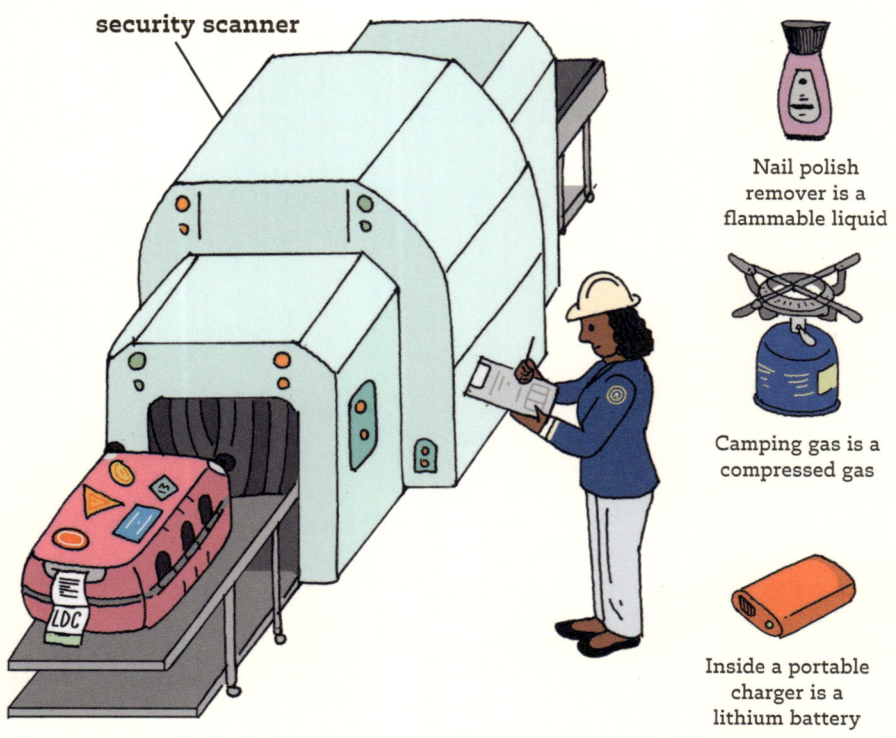

ARE BARCODES READ BY LASERS?

Laser beams and light curtains are used to scan the barcodes on printed luggage tags. Using this information, mechanical arms and gates redirect bags onto different tracks in the conveyor belt network. The information is also transmitted to **technicians** who from within a control room can track the whereabouts of any piece of luggage.

WHAT IF I CHECK IN EARLY?

When a bag is checked in early, it is flipped onto a plastic tray and moved to storage racks. Three hours before departure, the bag is automatically retrieved by cranes, returned to the network of conveyor belts, and directed to the correct flight. The early bags are usually last off the flight because they are loaded on first.

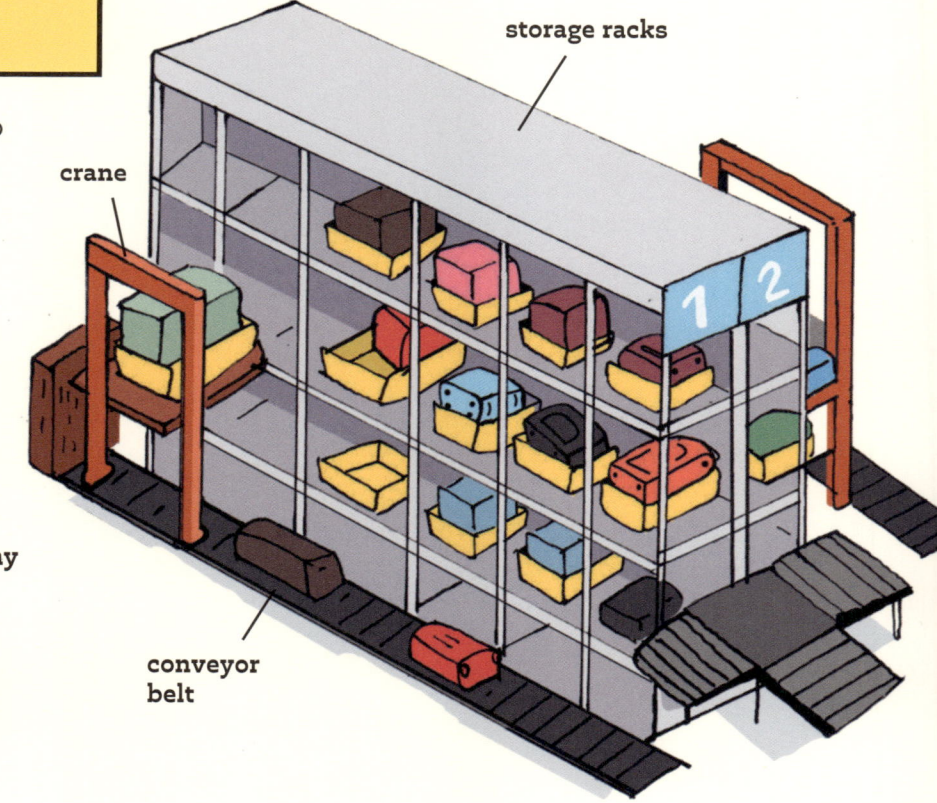

HOW FAR DOES MY BAG TRAVEL AROUND THE AIRPORT?

A luggage system is a large network of conveyor belts powered by motors. At Changi Airport in Singapore, the conveyor belts are located 262 feet underground, deeper than the underground metro train.

The conveyor belt tracks that connect Terminals 1, 2, and 3 are 8 miles long. Bags travel at a pace of 23 feet per second, which is faster than a human can run.

LUGGAGE & CARGO

WHY CAN'T I RIDE ON THE LUGGAGE CAROUSEL?

Technicians **monitor** the conveyor belt system from a control room using CCTV. If a bag falls off or gets stuck, they will know right away. They will also be able to see unidentified items in the luggage area, such as the child who rode the carousel at Atlanta Airport or the raccoon at Philadelphia Airport, both of whom had to be rescued.

CAN PIGS FLY?

Air travel was originally designed with humans in mind, but today many more objects—and animals—travel the world by air. Most passenger planes carry some form of **cargo** on them but special cargo calls for special flights. Cargo flights are solely dedicated to carrying a particular type of cargo. They tend to fly at night so they don't disrupt an airport's busy schedule.

snake

cushioning

heat pad

CAN I TAKE SNAKES ON A PLANE?

You can't take a snake with you on a passenger flight but you can transport it on a cargo flight. Air gets very cold at high altitudes, so cold-blooded reptiles like snakes need to be packed in a breathable crate with a heat pad to keep their blood temperature warm during the flight. Don't forget to lock the crate—nobody wants to encounter a snake on a plane!

breathable crate

padlock

CAN A PLANE FLY A PLANE?

The largest airplanes in the world are cargo planes built to carry trucks, boats, planes, and even spacecraft. Rather than have a small door in the side, the entire nose of a cargo plane, such as NASA's Super Guppy, opens on a hinge.

16

LUGGAGE & CARGO

DO YOU HAVE THE HEART?

When an organ donor dies, their organs are matched to someone in need of a transplant. A heart or a lung can only last up to ten hours outside of a body, so organ transport teams fly in a small jet to get to the patient quickly. Organs are stored on ice and carried in a cooling bin on the flight.

HOW DO LETTERS FLY AIR MAIL?

Small passenger planes are often converted into cargo planes after they have been in service for a number of years. They are ideal for carrying air mail letters and small packages around the world quickly.

HOW DO HORSES GET TO THE OLYMPICS?

Horses travel to international races and competitions in metal stalls strapped to the inside of a cargo plane. The stalls are narrow enough to stop the horses from falling over. A horse can suffer from travel sickness if it holds its head up for too long, so the front of the stalls are low enough for a horse to lower its head.

CAN A BODY SCANNER SEE ME NAKED?

Before boarding an airplane, all passengers and staff pass through airport security. Belongings and bodies are scanned to make sure no sharp objects or large volumes of liquid are taken into the plane's cabin. A body scanner cannot see you naked. It beams radio waves onto your body, which reflect off anything made of metal, and also detects unusual-looking objects. The image a security officer sees is a cartoon outline of a person. If you leave a pair of scissors in your left pocket, the cartoon will appear with a yellow flag over your left hip. The security officer then knows to ask you to empty your left pocket.

WHERE DOES ALL THE SHAMPOO GO?

Every year, airports **confiscate** tons of bottled liquids, aerosol cans, and sharp objects that are not allowed in a plane's cabin. In one year, Stansted Airport in London collected more than 23 tons of aerosol cans containing shaving cream, hair spray, and spray deodorants. That's the weight of 7,000 elephants! They also confiscated two tons of sharp objects, including scissors, screwdrivers, corkscrews, and playing darts. Many airports work with local charities to make sure confiscated toiletries don't go to waste.

WHAT CAN A SNIFFER DOG SMELL?

Dogs have an excellent sense of smell and can be trained to sniff out specific odors. Airport security uses sniffer dogs to identify luggage containing fresh food or plants. They can also be trained to smell dangerous or illegal substances including explosives and drugs. Most airports choose beagles—not because they are better at smelling but because they are very friendly.

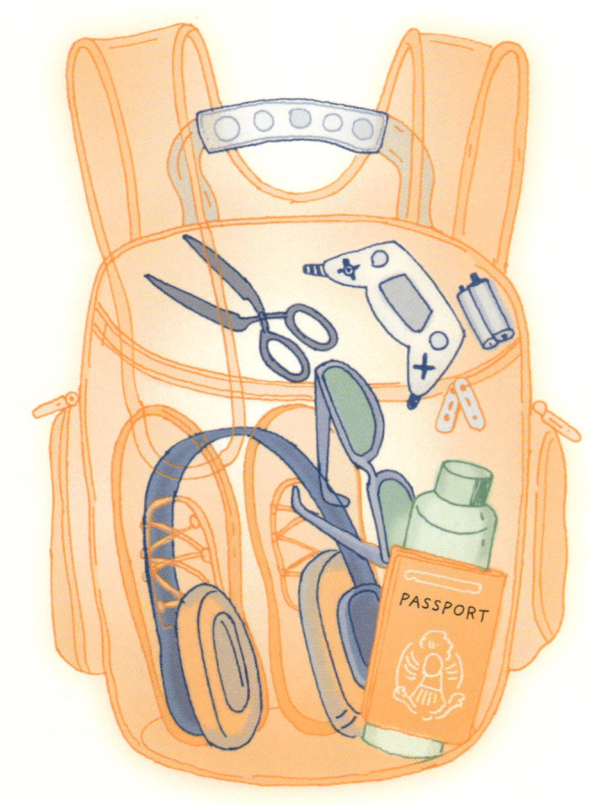

WHAT DOES AN X-RAY OF MY BACKPACK SHOW?

When your backpack goes through a luggage scanner, it is X-rayed from different angles. The colors that show up on the X-ray screen represent different types of materials—blue for metals, orange for cloth, and green for plastic. If you are carrying something dangerous, like a pair of scissors, they will show up as a blue scissor shape on the X-ray. Security will double check what they see by opening your bag.

DO BABIES NEED PASSPORTS?

Everybody who travels internationally needs a passport, including babies. Babies grow and change so quickly that it is sometimes easier to identify them by their fingerprint or a scan of their eye than it is from a photograph. A superthin electronic chip stored in the cover of your passport holds this information, which is known as "biometric data." It is the job of a passport controller to check that the data matches the person, or baby, in front of them.

WHY IS THERE A HOLOGRAM IN MY PASSPORT?

Holograms are one of many features that distinguish an official passport from a fake one. As well as checking that your passport is the right size and has the correct number of pages, a passport controller looks for things you can't see.

Invisible holograms and secret **watermarks** are printed on specific pages, and the stitching that holds the pages together turns a different color under UV light. Some passports also include numbers etched into thin layers of metal foil and patterns engraved on the pages themselves.

IS THE RAMP ACTUALLY A RAMP?

The area immediately outside the departure gate is called the "ramp"—but it isn't the type of sloping ramp you might be thinking of. It's usually buzzing with vehicles, zipping back and forth. While it may look chaotic, the ramp is under the careful control of the ground handling team, who work in all weathers and at all times of day to turn airplanes around within an hour of landing. Ramp agents and aircraft marshalers work quickly. To avoid crashes, they follow road markings on the ramp, and wear high-visibility clothing and use flashing lights to make sure they can be seen.

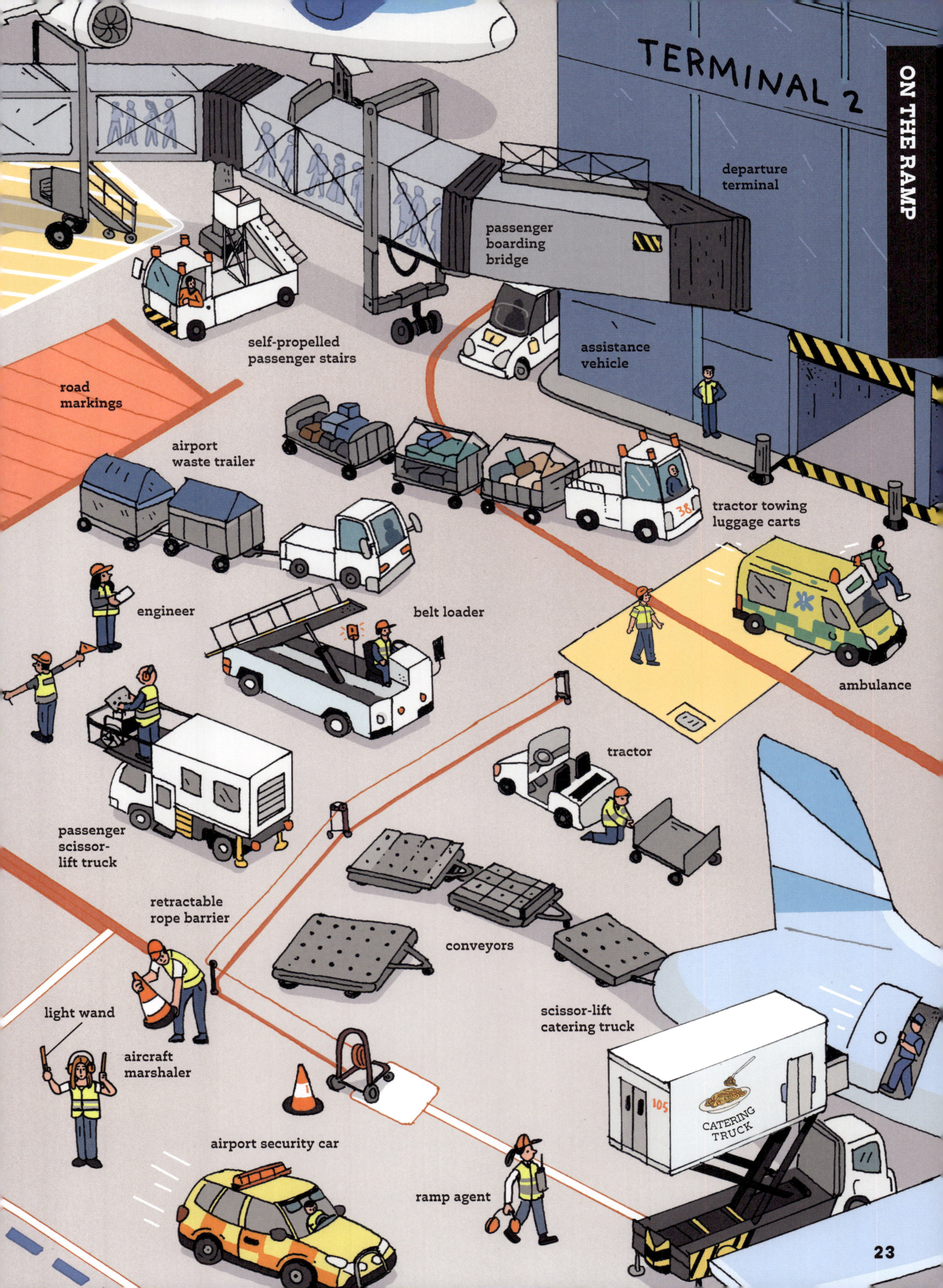

DOES A PLANE STOP AT A GAS STATION?

There isn't a gas station large enough to fill up all the planes at an airport. Instead, airports rely on fuel farms—large storage tanks at the edge of an airport runway that store thousands of gallons of jet fuel. Fuel farm tanks are connected by pipes to a pit under the ramp. Fuel trucks connect their hoses to these pipes and pump jet fuel up into the airplane's fuel tank, which is in its wings. Fuel is pumped in at a rate of 630 gallons per minute, and it takes around fifteen to twenty minutes to refuel a large aircraft.

| Turn right | Turn left | Start engines | Stop |

WHAT SIGNALS DOES AN AIRCRAFT MARSHALER SEND?

An aircraft marshaler's job is to guide the pilot when they are maneuvering the airplane on the ground. The marshaler's signals include instructions such as "straight ahead," "left," "right," "slow down," and "stop."

Aircraft marshalers carry a light wand in each hand so that their signals can be seen in all weathers and at all hours of the day. They are also responsible for inserting chocks under the airplane's wheels to prevent the plane from rolling when it is parked.

Emergency stop

Straight ahead

Cut engines

Slow down

ON THE RAMP

WHERE DOES ALL THE POOP GO?

Travelers can flush the toilet on a long-haul flight up to 1,000 times, producing up to 230 gallons of sewage. All of this waste is stored in a sealed tank at the rear of the plane. Each time a plane lands, a dedicated toilet waste truck empties the poop and pee from the plane. The truck has a vacuum hose that sucks out the waste into a tank so that it can be transported to a wastewater treatment plant—often on site at major airports—for processing and disposal.

WHO COOKS ALL THE MEALS?

In-flight meals are prepared by a team of chefs at a factory close to each airport. Hot foods, like curries and stews, are cooked in large batches and then frozen to keep them fresh. Cold foods are portioned and plated up before being stored in a refrigerator. Catering staff prepare the meal trays in advance, with utensils and napkins, before loading everything into carts. Carts are transported in large refrigerated scissor-lift trucks onto the ramp where they are lifted up into the airplane.

WHY IS THAT AIRPLANE BEING TOWED?

The **thrust** on an airplane's engine creates a high-speed wind that can turn even the smallest items into dangerous **projectiles**. Engines are also very noisy and use a lot of fuel. Pushback tow tractors, or "tugs," are used to move an airplane off the ramp so that it can start its engines away from ramp equipment. Tow tractors are also essential for pushing a plane backward because an airplane doesn't have a reverse gear.

WHAT DOES THAT VEHICLE DO?

Vehicles at an airport are engineered with very specific tasks in mind. The people who drive these vehicles are all part of the ground handling team. The vehicles are parked around the edge of the ramp area and spring into action as soon as a plane pulls up.

When it is driving along the ramp, the **SCISSOR-LIFT CATERING TRUCK** looks like a regular truck. But after it has parked and put down its stabilizers, watch it lift the refrigerated storage unit three times its original height!

A **SELF-PROPELLED STAIR** is an open-topped vehicle with a staircase on top. Designs vary and include a version that can extend and retract its staircase, adapting to the height of different airplanes.

The **BELT LOADER** is a mobile conveyor belt that is raised and lowered by a piston. Luggage handlers standing on the ramp place luggage on the belt, which carries it up to the airplane's **hold** where a specialist air load manager is waiting to receive it.

balcony

The **PASSENGER SCISSOR-LIFT TRUCK** has a tray at the back that lowers to the ground for wheelchair users, families with strollers, and people with limited mobility. The tray raises passengers to truck level and then transports them across the ramp. The body of the truck then rises to the level of the cabin door where a balcony extends outward. The passengers don't have to climb any steps to get onto the airplane.

ON THE RAMP

extendable hose arm

AIRPORT RESCUE AND FIREFIGHTING VEHICLES have water hoses mounted onto both the front bumper and an extendable arm, which can be operated safely from inside the cab of the truck. Airport fire engines can produce over 15,000 gallons of foam per minute and aim it through doorways, over wings, or even directly into the cabin without leaving the safety of the cab. These vehicles are also equipped with thermal imaging cameras to detect hot areas or fires on an aircraft that may not be visible from outside.

WHAT DOES THIS SWITCH DO?

The plane is controlled from the cockpit. On a large passenger aircraft, this area is called the flight deck. The pilot—known as the captain—sits on the left, with the copilot—or first officer—on the right. Older aircraft were controlled with buttons, switches, and dials, but today many of these have been replaced with computers and digital displays. One important flight instrument is the altimeter, which shows the height of the plane. Another is the vertical speed indicator, which displays how quickly the plane is moving up or down. Both of these instruments are now usually shown on the flight deck's digital displays. You'll still find hundreds of other switches and controls in most modern cockpits, but many of them are only for use in specific emergencies. Pilots can go their whole career without touching some of them.

IN THE COCKPIT

WHAT HAPPENS IF A PILOT GETS STUCK IN THE COCKPIT?

Some aircraft have an escape hatch in the roof of the cockpit. If the pilots get trapped inside the cockpit in an emergency, they can use the hatch to escape. There's also a rope to help them climb down the plane.

- overhead control panel
- head-up display
- first officer
- autopilot control panel
- multifunction display
- yoke (steering wheel)
- thrust lever
- sheepskin seat cover

Four bars = Captain

Three bars = First Officer

WHY DO PILOTS WEAR UNIFORMS?

Pilots wear uniforms so that they are easily identifiable to passengers and cabin crew. Their clothes are smart and professional, and were originally inspired by the outfits of naval officers. The uniform usually consists of a brimmed hat, a suit jacket, and a shirt and tie. Stripes on the cuff of the jacket, as well as the epaulet—a decorative detail found on the shoulders of the shirt—show the experience of an officer: three stripes for a first officer and four for a captain.

WHO FLIES THE PLANE WHEN THE PILOT NEEDS THE BATHROOM?

The captain is usually the person with the most flying experience, and has overall responsibility for the aircraft and everyone on board. However, the first officer is also a fully trained pilot, and they take turns to fly the plane. For safety, there must be two people in the flight deck at all times, so while a pilot goes to the bathroom, a member of the **cabin crew** steps into the room. Many precautions are taken to make sure that there's always someone able to fly the plane. For example, the captain and copilot don't eat the same things. If one has food poisoning from their meal, the other will still be well enough to be at the helm.

WHY DO THE COCKPIT DOORS STAY CLOSED?

For the safety of all on board, only authorized people have access to the cockpit, and the door to it is locked for the entirety of a flight. Members of cabin crew must speak to the captain via radio to request access, and usually there's a camera outside the door to verify a person's identity before they can be admitted. It can also be unlocked by typing a code into a keypad. The door to the cockpit is sturdy and secure—it's built from steel and is also fireproof.

IN THE COCKPIT

CAN THE PILOT SEE IN THE DARK?

The pilot doesn't need to see in the dark to fly the plane—in fact, they don't even need to look out of the window. Instead, pilots rely on flight instruments that measure the plane's airspeed, altitude, direction, and even how level the plane is. However, pilots do need to look out of the plane during takeoff and landing, especially at night or during bad weather. They use the lights on and around the runway to judge where they are.

CAN A PLANE FLY ITSELF?

One of the computer systems on a plane is known as the autopilot. Once the flight plan is uploaded to it, the autopilot can automatically fly the plane to its destination. The autopilot also communicates with sensors on the outside of the plane to check that everything is working as it should be. Today, the autopilot must be monitored by the captain and first officer, and it still has to be told things like when the plane should climb or descend. Most takeoffs and landings are still controlled manually by a pilot, but in the future it's possible that autopilot could fly planes without the need for humans!

HOW DO PILOTS KNOW HOW MUCH FUEL THEY NEED?

Before an aircraft takes to the sky, flight planners calculate the essential amount of fuel needed for the journey. The captain, with the help of the first officer, then decides how much extra fuel will be needed. The pilots examine all factors that might affect the flight—such as poor weather conditions that could make the journey longer—and will decide on the final amount of fuel that the plane should be loaded with before takeoff.

WHAT DO AIR TRAFFIC CONTROLLERS DO?

The control tower is a tall building in the grounds of the airport. Inside, a group of air traffic controllers work together as a team. They coordinate the movements of airplanes around the aiport's **taxiways** and runways, and in the sky above. By talking to pilots via radio and using several computers, they give permission for safe takeoffs and landings. They plan the order in which planes move around, and also make sure that aircraft and other vehicles travel safely around the **airfield**. It's a tiring and busy job that takes much concentration and a lot of multitasking, so the manager of the control tower makes sure that everyone on the air traffic control team takes a break every two hours.

WHAT CAN YOU SEE FROM THE CONTROL TOWERS?

Air traffic controllers have an eagle-eyed view from the high room in which they sit because it's completely covered in windows—with a full 360-degree view of the runways and the sky. But **radar** technology also shows the location of aircraft on their computer screens, which is useful when there's poor visibility due to bad weather. And sometimes, a good old pair of binoculars helps, too!

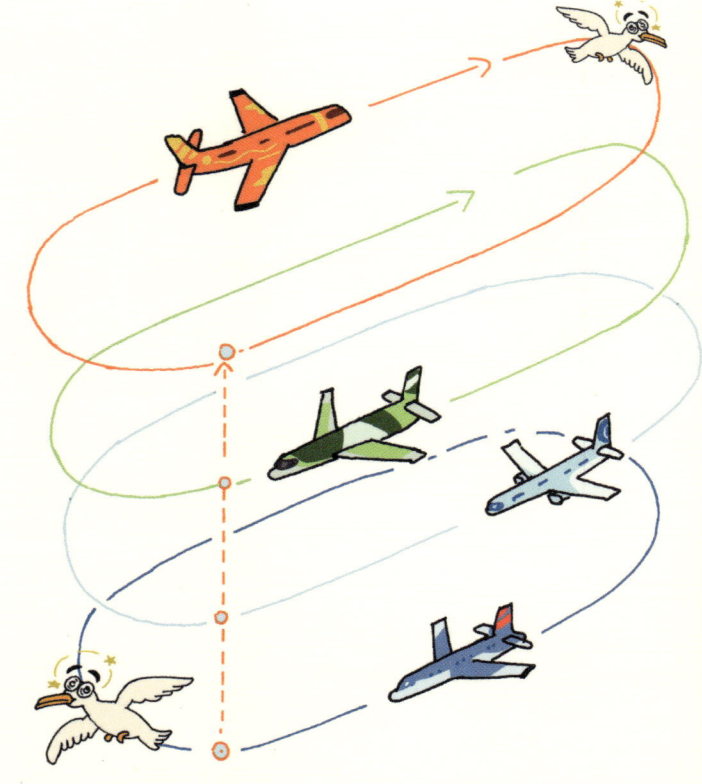

DO PLANES GET STUCK IN TRAFFIC JAMS?

Air traffic controllers carefully plan the movements of planes to make sure there are no delays. But if there's bad weather or a problem with the runway, an aircraft has to wait for its turn to land. Unlike cars on a road, planes can't just stop in mid-air, so air traffic control will tell them to enter a holding pattern. This means the aircraft will fly around and around an oval-shaped flight path above an airport until it's cleared for landing. If there's more than one plane, they will fly in holding patterns on top of each other. This is called a "stack." It's like a traffic jam in the sky!

HOW DO AIR TRAFFIC CONTROLLERS COMMUNICATE WITH PILOTS?

When a plane is in airspace managed by an airport, either on the ground or in the sky, the pilot and an air traffic controller will talk via radio. To keep communication clear and brief, pilots and controllers use a lot of precise words when talking. For example, the word "Roger" means that you've received and understood a message.

"Roger that!"

"Who's Roger?"

CAN AIR TRAFFIC CONTROLLERS CONTROL THE WEATHER?

No . . . but an air traffic controller is a pilot's best chance of taking off and landing safely in any kind of weather. They have access to equipment that uses radar technology to show how much precipitation—or water in the sky—is in the nearby airspace. During poor weather, air traffic controllers will make decisions on the safest course of action. Heavy snow, wind, or rain could make a journey dangerous. Controllers will decide whether planes should be "grounded," meaning they're stopped from taking to the skies until the weather has cleared up.

THE CONTROL TOWER

HOW MANY PLANES ARE IN THE AIR AT ONE TIME?

At any one time, there are thousands of flights in the air, but the total number varies and can be anywhere from 8,000 to 20,000. Hartsfield-Jackson Atlanta Airport in Georgia can have up to 2,500 planes take off and land in just one day.

WHICH SIDE OF THE ROAD DO PLANES DRIVE ON?

An airport is filled with roads that are painted with markings. Taxiways are the smaller paths with yellow markings that planes use to move to different areas of the airfield. Runways are the superlong stretches for takeoffs and landings. Only one aircraft will travel on a runway at once. Even large airports might only have one runway because it's possible for many planes to take off and land from the same runway quickly if it's well-managed by air traffic control.

Unlike a regular road, there is no right or left side on a runway. Instead, it is the perfect width for an aircraft to travel down the middle. Planes can use either end of the runway to take off or land, and this depends on many factors, including the plane's path of travel, the direction of the wind, and the size of the aircraft. The runway is lined with lights as a guide at night or through poor weather conditions.

HOLDING POSITION
These yellow lines show where a plane must stop until it's told to move onto the runway by air traffic control.

THRESHOLD
These striped lines mark the starting point of the runway for landing. The number of stripes indicate the width of the runway.

BLAST PAD
This area is used to contain the force of jet engine blasts before takeoff. It also provides an emergency overrun area if an aircraft takes longer to takeoff or land than it should.

13,000 ft.

HOW LONG IS THE RUNWAY?

The length of a runway can vary. Big, heavy airliner jets, such as the Airbus A380, take longer to get to takeoff speed than smaller planes, so runways in a commercial airport can be very long—between 8,000 and 13,000 feet. Airports at places of high elevation also have long runways because the air is thinner there, meaning that a plane takes much longer to get to takeoff speed.

But some runways can be very small, too—Juancho E. Yrausquin in Saba, Caribbean Netherlands, has one of the smallest runways in the world at only 1,300 feet long. Only pilots with special training can land on it.

1,300 ft.

DO RUNWAYS GET RUN DOWN?

Over 500 planes land on Frankfurt Airport's runways everyday. This constant use wears down the runways, so they have to be regularly replaced. To prevent holding up air traffic, workers replace a runway in sections. First, diggers break up the old concrete and **asphalt** that the surface is made of and remove 1,650 tons of rubble. The area is then flattened to a depth of 27.5 inches below the runway surface. A foundation of recycled concrete is then spread evenly across the section. Tubes to house electrical cables for runway lighting are laid down. Three layers of hot asphalt are then poured over the section and flattened with a steam roller. Paint markings are added. Sand is sprayed over the cooling asphalt to seal any gaps and lastly, a cleaning truck sweeps the surface clean. It takes eight hours to replace one section of runway.

ON THE RUNWAY

DOES A RUNWAY NEED CLEANING?

Every time a plane skids to a halt on a runway, it leaves behind rubber from its tires, sometimes up to 70 pounds of it. It's really important that this debris is cleaned away as often as possible, otherwise a buildup of the rubber can stop planes from landing safely. Commercial airports clean their runways between three and five times per week. Special vehicles drive up and down during a cleaning session, which usually happens in the middle of the night when there are no scheduled flights. The vans are equipped with high-pressure water jets that blast the runway to clean it. The vans collect the waste water too, so that the runway is ready for action right away.

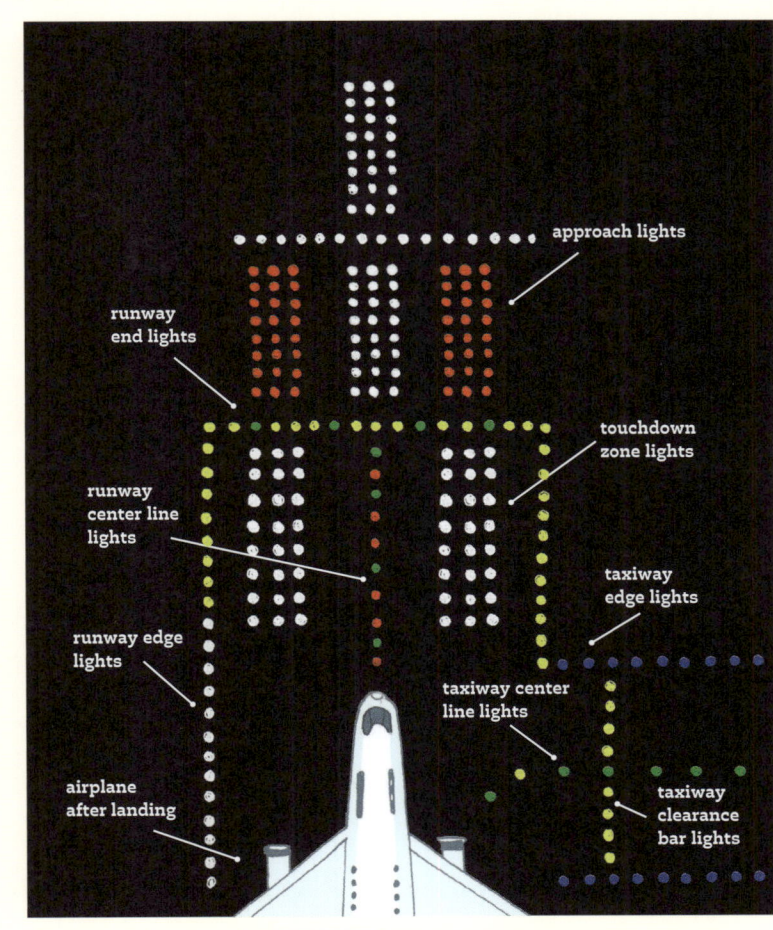

ARE THERE TRAFFIC LIGHTS ON THE RUNWAY?

During the night or in cases of poor visibility due to bad weather, a patchwork of different lights help to guide a pilot's way across the airfield. The edge of the runway is marked with white or yellow lights. The center line lights are white, too. The start of the runway is marked with green lights, while the end is marked with red. Blue and green lights guide a pilot along the taxiways.

WHAT DIRECTION DO RUNWAYS POINT?

Runways will usually be built in the direction that takes advantage of the prevailing wind—the strongest direction of wind in the area. It helps to give the plane a lift into the sky!

39

DO ANIMALS LIVE AT AIRPORTS?

Airports are built on the edge of cities where there are large expanses of land. Wild animals can't resist feeding and nesting in the long grass near **perimeter fences**, or lying on the runways to absorb the heat of the day. The problem is that planes and animals don't really mix . . .

Every June and July turtle patrols at JFK Airport in New York City keep an eye out for diamondback terrapins. The terrapins wander across the runway in search of higher ground to lay their eggs on, away from high ocean tides in Jamaica Bay.

Wild hares live in burrows next to the runway at Milan Linate Airport in Italy. The hares block takeoffs and landings, and cause problems with the sensors that monitor the airport. So, each year volunteers chase the hares into nets and transfer them to a local wildlife reserve.

WOULD I GET AN ELECTRIC SHOCK IF I TOUCHED THE PERIMETER FENCE?

No—the electromagnetic waves that pass through a perimeter fence are used to detect movement rather than to electrify anything that touches it. Sharp wires along the tall fence are enough to deter people from entering, but many animals find a way to slip through the net . . .

ON THE RUNWAY

Heathrow Airport in London uses wild goose sounds to scare off seagulls. The force of a gull hitting a plane flying at 300 miles per hour is like dropping a ton of concrete from the roof of a two story house. It's not good for either the bird or the airplane.

A seal weighing 440 pounds had to be removed from the runway of Wiley Post-Will Rogers Memorial Airport in Alaska after heavy storms. The runway was a warm and calm spot to sunbathe. Air traffic resumed after the seal was transported away on a sled.

Orlando International Airport in Florida is surrounded by lakes, ponds, and waterways, which are home to alligators. Occasionally, an alligator will delay a flight by walking across the taxiway to get to a pond.

Deer have been known to squeeze their way through perimeter fences to graze on the grass along the runway at Baltimore/Washington International Airport in Maryland. Airport employees scare them away by slowly driving trucks toward them with the sirens on.

WHY CAN'T WE FLY WITH THE WINDOWS OPEN?

Airplanes fly thousands of feet high up in the air, where the air temperature is between -58°F and -94°F—that's freezing cold! The cabin is sealed tight before the airplane takes off to create an environment that is comfortable to fly in. The plane's air conditioning draws fresh air in from the outside and heats it up to a comfortable temperature. On a long-haul flight, the cabin crew turn up the temperature after dinner to help passengers fall asleep, and chill the temperature to wake everyone up for breakfast.

ON BOARD THE PLANE

- overhead compartment
- window
- vomit bag
- armrest
- pillow
- TV screen
- blanket
- tray table
- inflight magazine
- eye mask
- dinner tray

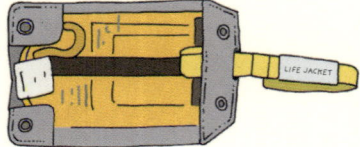
life jacket pack

cabin crew demonstration
- mouth inflation tube
- light
- inflation toggle

WHO CHECKS WHETHER THE LIFE JACKETS WORK?

Every plane is fitted with safety equipment in case of an emergency. Life jackets are stored under each passenger's seat or in the panel above their head. A sample number of life jackets are checked by cabin crew before every flight, and they are fully inspected during an aircraft's annual checks. Cabin safety inspectors look for signs of damage, and general wear and tear. Life jackets are made from long-lasting materials, but to be extra safe, they are given an expiration date and replaced every ten years. Those used by Hawaiian Airlines are upcycled into waterproof bags used by surfers to keep their belongings dry.

I THINK I'M GOING TO BE SICK . . .

Flying can have all kinds of effects on the human body. Once you're up in the air, one third of your taste buds will stop working, you'll be more likely to cry at movies, yours ears might "pop" during takeoff and landing and, if you're really unlucky, you might suffer from air sickness. There is a waterproof vomit bag in the pocket of the seat in front of you. If you start to feel queasy, pull it out and let a flight attendant know you're not feeling well. Take regular sips of cold water and focus your eyes on the horizon.

WHY DO I FEEL LIKE FARTING?

Have you ever noticed that your bag of chips or bottle of water starts to swell up on a flight? The same thing happens in your intestine and stomach. The gas in your guts expands as the **air pressure** around you decreases, which means you're more likely to fart once your plane is airborne. But being at a high altitude—a great height above sea level—also has its advantages. There is plenty of fresh air to air condition the plane with and high altitude air is so dry, it makes it harder for everyone to smell. Phew!

ON BOARD THE PLANE

WILL THE TOILET SUCK MY INSIDES OUT?

The vacuum that sucks an airplane toilet clean may make a loud noise but it isn't strong enough to suck the organs out of your body. Pee and poop in an airplane toilet is sucked away by a strong vacuum, rather than being flushed away by water for a couple of reasons. Firstly, toilet water (and waste) would slosh everywhere during a patch of turbulence or bumpiness. Secondly, water is very heavy and would add too much weight to the plane.

CAN I PLAY SOCCER IN THE AISLE?

Weight in an airplane is carefully spread across the whole aircraft, from the luggage in the hold to the seating arrangements of the passengers. After the plane has taken off, you can move around the cabin but it is best to stay in your seat. Unlike in a car, which moves forward and backward, the main movement you experience on a plane is up and down. If the plane suddenly loses a lot of height, the ceiling will come down on your head. There are advantages to being strapped into your seat! Best to save the soccer game for when you're on the ground.

WHO CHOOSES THE MOVIES?

On long-haul flights, each seat has a small TV screen built into the back of it and every passenger is given a set of headphones. You'll be able to choose from a selection of movies and TV shows that are put together by a company that specializes in content for airlines. Because everyone's screens are visible, they prioritize family-friendly movies. Most flyers choose to watch a Hollywood blockbuster or a comedy series if they're watching TV. The selection changes each month, so if you don't want to get bored, fly out in one calendar month and fly back the next.

45

GLOSSARY

air pressure the weight of the air pushing down on Earth's surface. The air pressure decreases the higher you get above Earth's surface because the air particles weigh less, and have less air pushing down on them from above.

airfield an open area where aircraft can take off and land.

asphalt a smooth material often used as a surface for roads and airport runways. It is made of crushed stone, sand, and gravel bound together with sticky, waterproof tar.

boarding getting onto an airplane.

cabin crew a team of people whose job it is to help airplane passengers have a safe, comfortable flight. They are also called flight attendants.

cargo something nonhuman transported on an airplane.

check-in you can usually check in online before your flight, or at a check-in desk or self-service machine at the airport. It lets the airline know that you're planning to take the flight.

confiscate to take something away from someone, often because it's against the rules for them to have it.

conveyor belt a continuously moving strip that carries along objects placed on top of it.

database server a central computer or device that manages a lot of information, and sends it out to other computers in a network.

duty free you can often shop duty free at an airport, meaning that you don't pay the usual taxes (extra money) on what you buy.

hold the part of a passenger airplane where luggage and cargo is kept.

hologram a picture, typically created by lasers, that looks 3D rather than flat.

long-haul flight a flight that lasts several hours, typically six or more, and covers a very long distance.

monitor to continuously and carefully watch and check something.

perimeter fence a fence built all around the edge of an area of land.

projectile an object thrown forward very forcefully.

radar a system that can sense where objects are, and how fast they are moving, even in darkness or bad weather. One part of the system sends out radio waves that bounce off objects they hit. The waves travel back to a different part, which measures them.

taxiway a path, smaller than a runway, that airplanes use to move around different areas of the airfield.

technician a person whose job it is to use and look after machines or other specialized equipment.

terminal a building at an airport where passengers go before their flight, or exit through after their flight.

thrust the force generated by an aircraft's engines to move it through the air.

watermark a design formed in paper while it is being produced. It is often only visible when the paper is held up to the light.

INDEX

air mail 17
air pressure 44, 46
air traffic control 32-33, 34-35, 36
aircraft 22, 23, 24, 28, 29, 30, 31, 32, 34, 36, 45
airfield 32, 36, 39, 46
airline 8, 11, 44
    Hawaiian Airlines 44
airplane 8, 10, 11, 16, 17, 19, 22, 24, 25, 26, 27, 28-29, 30-31, 32, 34, 35, 36, 38, 39, 41, 42-43, 44-45
    Airbus A380 38
    Super Guppy 16
airports
    Frankfurt Airport, Germany 38
    Hartsfield-Jackson Atlanta Airport, Georgia 15, 35
    Heathrow Airport, London, UK 41
    John F. Kennedy (JFK) International Airport, New York City 6, 40
    Juancho E. Yrausquin Airport, Saba, Caribbean Netherlands 38
    Milan Linate Airport, Italy 40
    Orlando International Airport, Florida 41
    Philadelphia Airport, Pennsylvania 15
    Singapore Changi Airport, Singapore 6, 15
    Wiley Post-Will Rogers Memorial Airport, Alaska 41
airspace 34, 35
animals 15, 16, 17, 18, 20, 40-41
arrivals 7, 13
autopilot 29, 31

bag 9, 13, 14, 15, 18, 20, 23, 28, 43, 44
bathroom 9, 42
biometric data 19, 21
boarding 7, 8, 11, 19, 23, 46

cabin 19, 20, 27, 42-43, 44-45
cabin crew 30, 42, 43, 44, 46
cargo 13, 16-17, 46
CCTV 9, 15
check-in 8, 9, 10, 12, 13, 14
chocks 22, 24
cleaning 38, 39,
copilot (first officer) 28, 30, 31
cockpit 28-29, 30-31
computer 28, 31, 32, 34
control tower 7, 32-33, 34-35
conveyor belt 12, 13, 14, 15, 18, 26, 46

dangerous items 14, 20
departures 7, 8-9, 10-11, 12
duty free 10, 46

emergency 24, 28, 29, 31, 36, 44
explosive detection system machine (EDS) 14

flight attendant 30, 42, 43, 44
flight deck 28, 30
flight instruments 28, 31
flight path 34
food 20, 25, 26, 42
fuel 22, 23, 24, 25, 31, 36

gate (departure gate) 11, 22, 25
ground handling team 22, 26

hold (luggage hold) 26, 43, 45
holding pattern 34

information board 8

jobs at the airport
    air load manager 26
    air traffic controller 32-33, 34-35, 36
    aircraft marshaler 7, 22, 23, 24
    airport operations controller 9
    cabin safety inspector 44
    flight planner 31
    luggage handler 13, 26
    passport controller 19, 21
    ramp agent 22, 23
    security officer 18, 19
    security operator 12, 14
    technician 14, 15

landing 22, 25, 31, 32, 34, 35, 36, 37, 38, 39, 40, 44
lighting 22, 31, 32, 36, 38, 39, 42
long-haul flight 6, 25, 43, 45
luggage 8, 9, 12-13, 14-15, 18, 20, 23, 26, 43, 45

NASA 16

organs 17, 4

passengers 6, 10, 16, 17, 19, 22, 23, 27, 28, 30, 42-43, 44-45
passport 10, 19, 21
perimeter fence 7, 40, 41, 46
pilot 24, 25, 28, 29, 30, 31, 32, 34, 35, 37, 38, 39

radar 33, 34, 35
radio 30, 32, 33, 34
ramp 7, 22-23, 24-25, 26-27
road markings 22, 23, 36-37, 38
runway 7, 24, 25, 31, 32, 33, 34, 36-37, 38-39, 40-41

safety 22, 27, 30, 31, 32, 35, 39, 42, 44
scanner 12, 14, 18, 19, 20, 21
security 10, 12, 14, 18-19, 20, 23
sensors 13, 31, 40
sewage 25
shuttle cart 9, 11
sickness 17, 43, 44
sniffer dog 18, 20
storage 13, 14, 24, 26
suitcase (luggage) 8, 9, 12-13, 14-15, 18, 20, 23, 26, 43, 45

takeoff 11, 31, 32, 36, 38, 40
tarmac 22, 25, 26, 27, 38
taxiway 7, 11, 32, 36, 39, 41
terminal 6, 7, 8-9, 10-11, 12-13, 15, 23
time zones 10
toilet 22, 25, 45
TV 43, 45

vehicles 22-23, 26-27, 32, 39
    airport rescue and firefighting vehicles 7, 22, 27
    belt loader 6, 22, 26
    fuel tanker (fuel truck) 6-7, 23, 24
    passenger scissor-lift truck 22, 27
    pushback tow tractor ("tug") 6, 22, 25
    scissor-lift catering truck 6, 23, 25, 26
    self-propelled passenger stairs 7, 23, 26
    toilet waste truck 22, 25

weather 24, 31, 34, 35, 36, 39
wind 25, 35, 36, 39
window 31, 33, 34, 43

X-rays 14, 20

ABOUT THE CONSULTANT

Laurence Hardisty is a pilot who has been flying commercial aircraft for thirteen years. He is an airline line training captain, as well as an advisor to the Manchester Airports Group (MAG) development committee, working to improve airport flow and efficiency and airport/airline cooperation.

ABOUT THE ILLUSTRATOR

Maxim Usik is no stranger to airports! After working in design studios in Helsinki he became a freelance illustrator and took off on a world tour, working remotely for clients while exploring South America, Asia, and Europe.

Airports © 2026 Thames & Hudson Ltd, London

Text © 2026 Thames & Hudson Ltd, London
Illustrations © 2026 Maxim Usik
Consultancy by Laurence Hardisty
With special thanks to Louis Elfari

All Rights Reserved. No part of this publication may be reproduced or transmitted in any form or by any means, electronic or mechanical, including photocopy, recording, or any other information storage and retrieval system, without prior permission in writing from the publisher.

First published in 2026 in the United States of America by Thames & Hudson Inc., 500 Fifth Avenue, New York, New York 10110

EU Authorized Representative: Interart S.A.R.L.
19 rue Charles Auray, 93500 Pantin, Paris, France
productsafety@thameshudson.co.uk
interart.fr

Library of Congress Control Number 2024937738

ISBN 978-0-500-65387-6
01

Printed and bound in China by C&C Offset Printing Co. Ltd

Be the first to know about our new releases, exclusive content, and author events by visiting
thamesandhudson.com
thamesandhudsonusa.com
thamesandhudson.com.au